BASTARD SERIES

Amusing Swear Words To Color

For Stress Releasing

By

Queenie McJody

Happy Coloring!

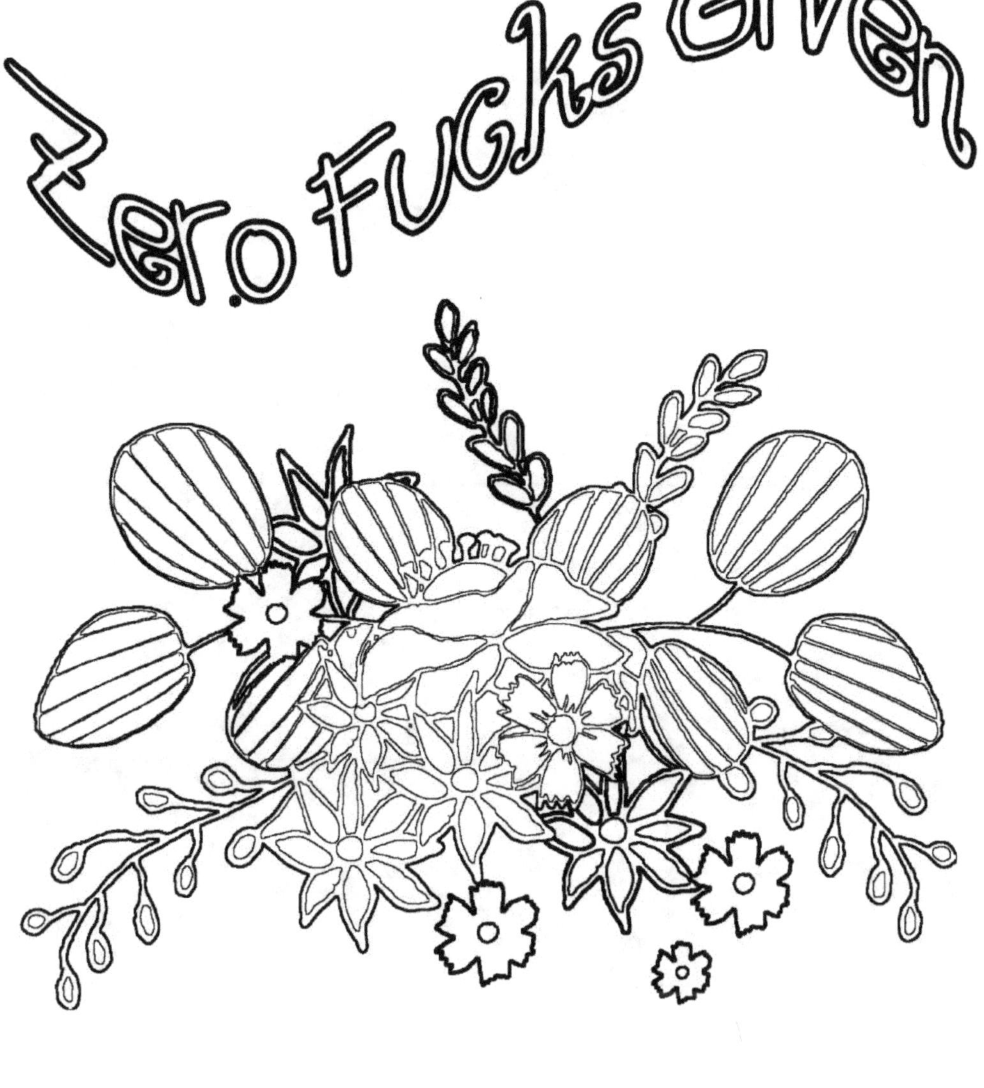
Zero Fucks Given

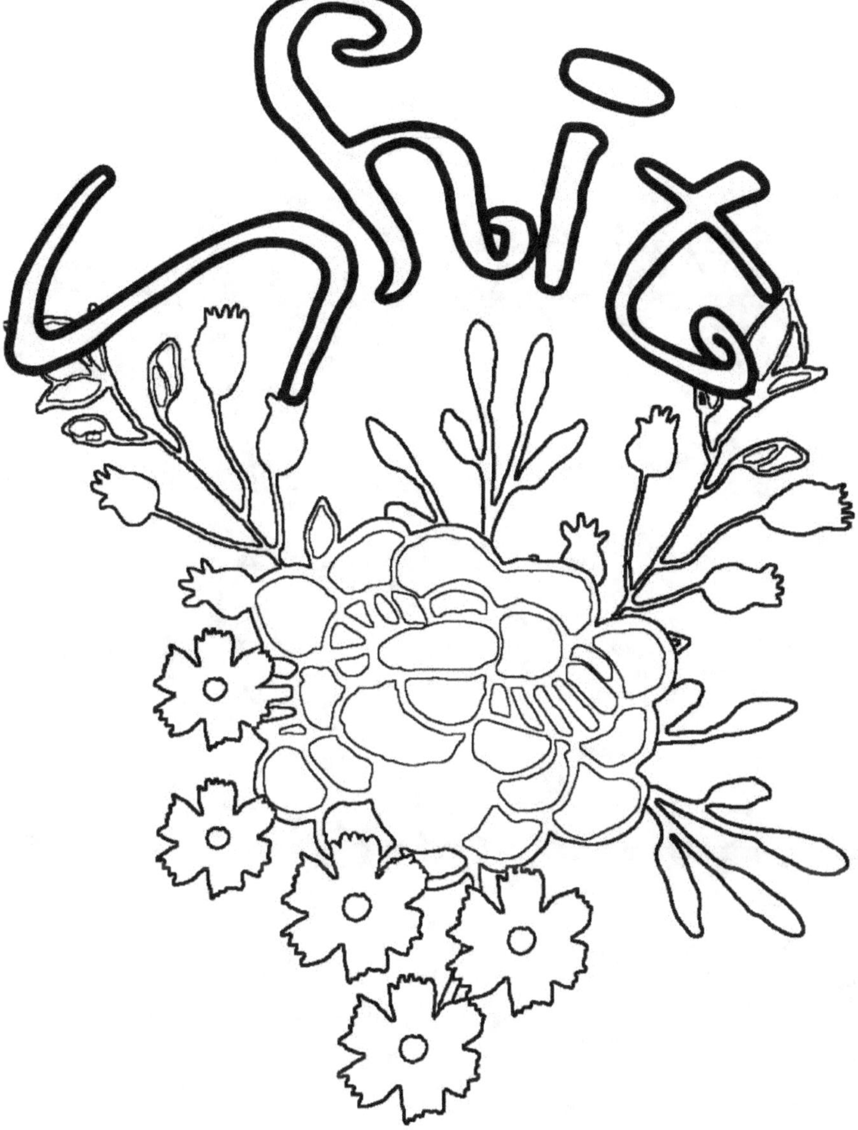
Shit

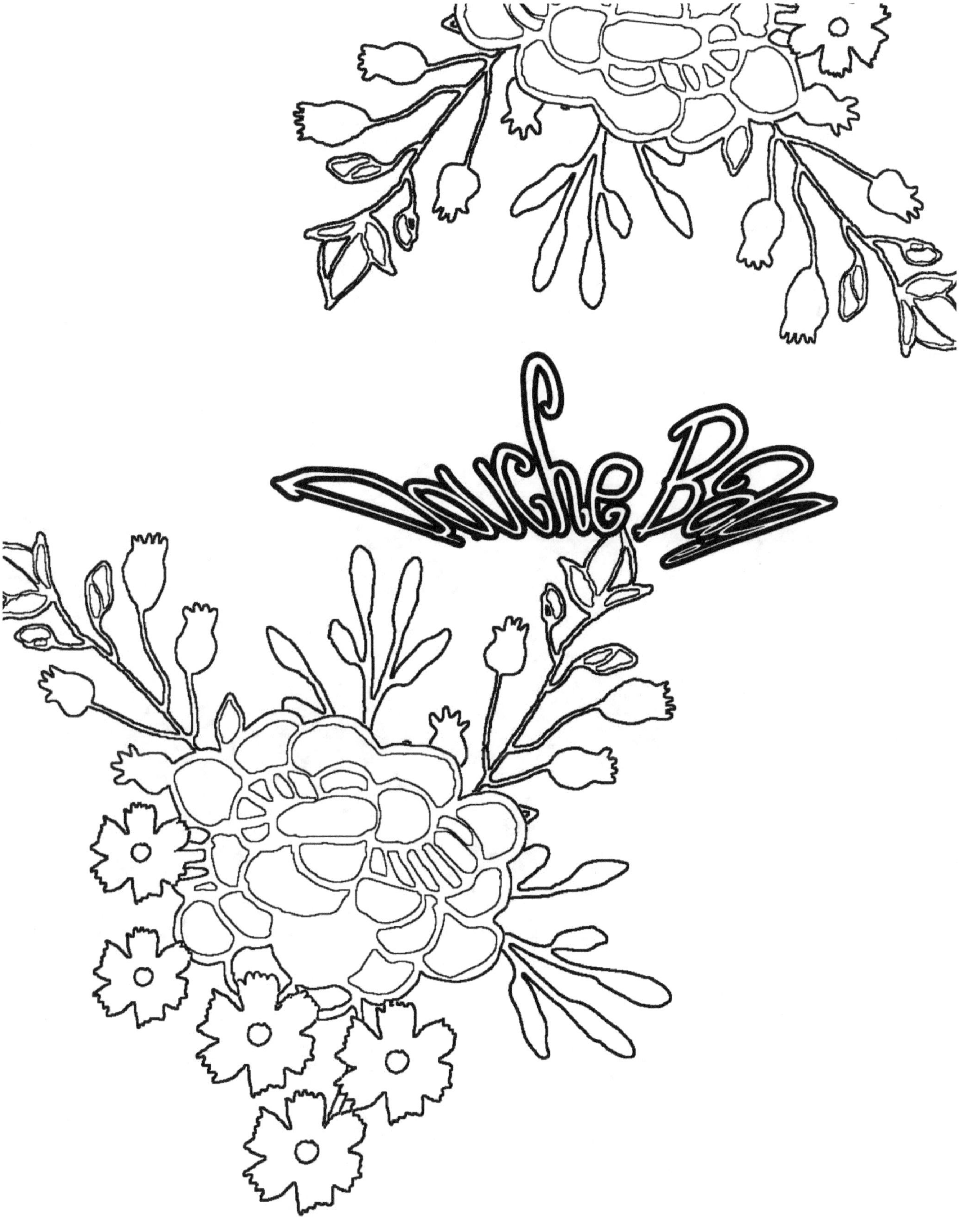
Douche Bag

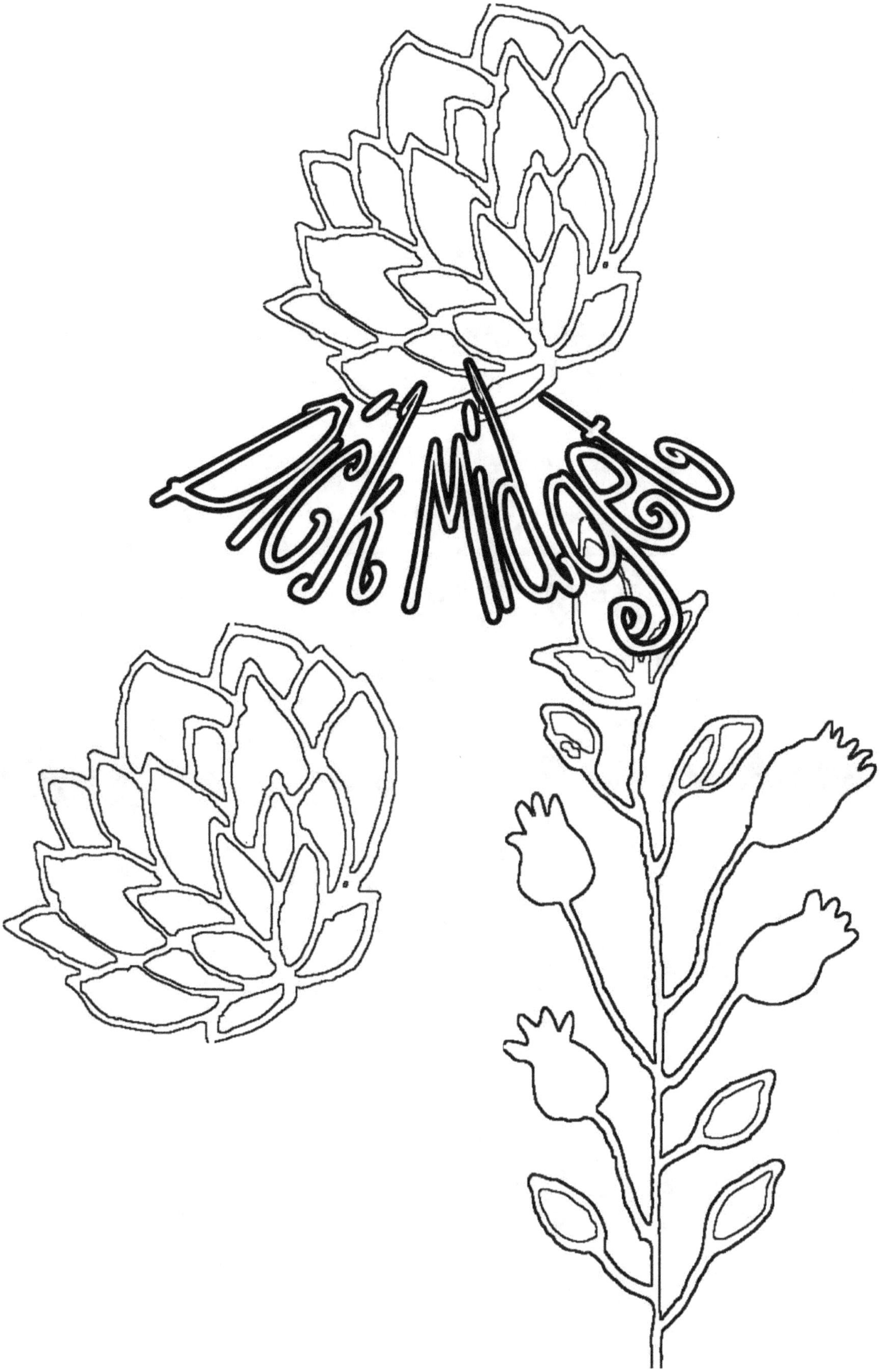
Dick Midget

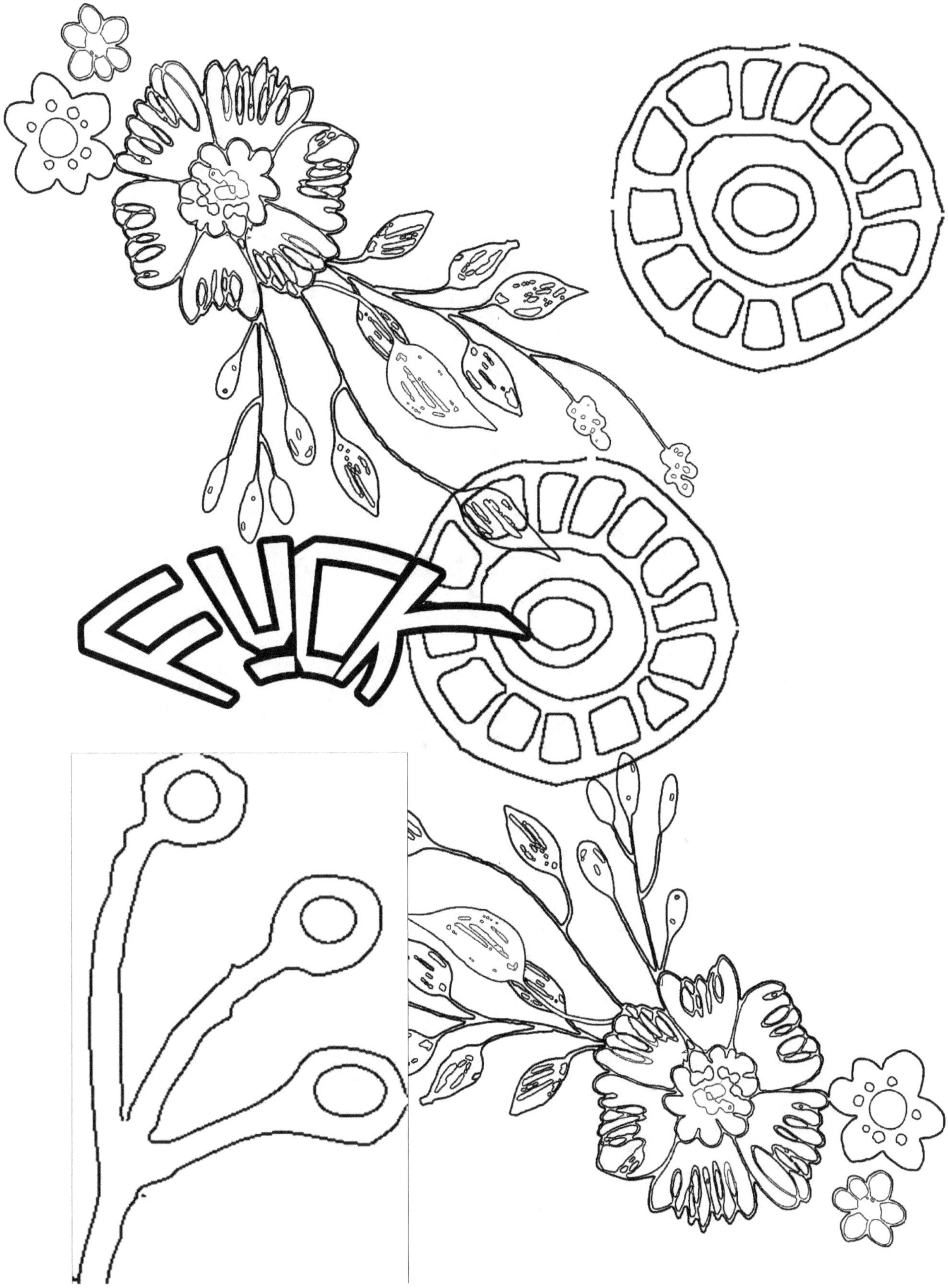
FUCK

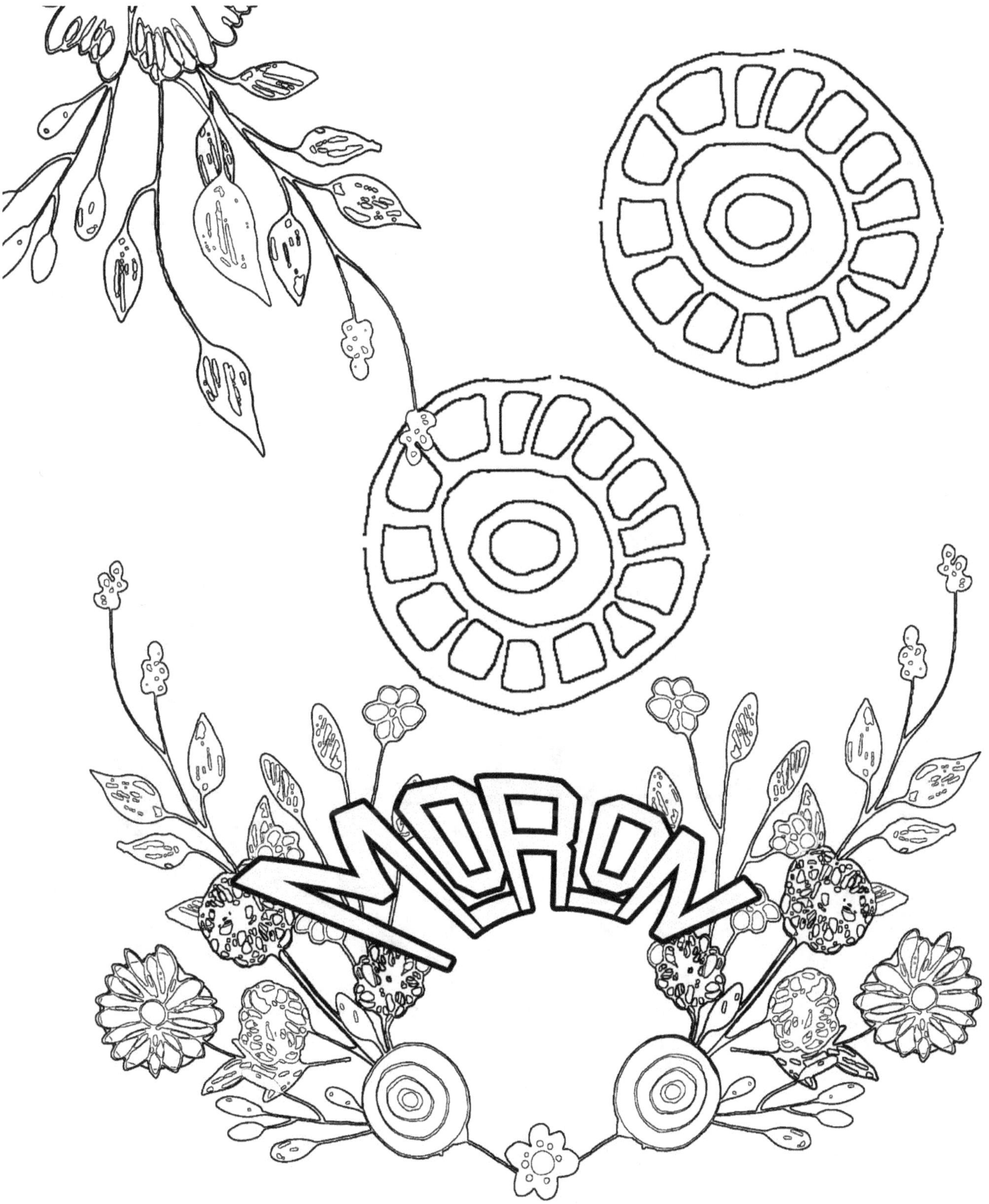
MORON

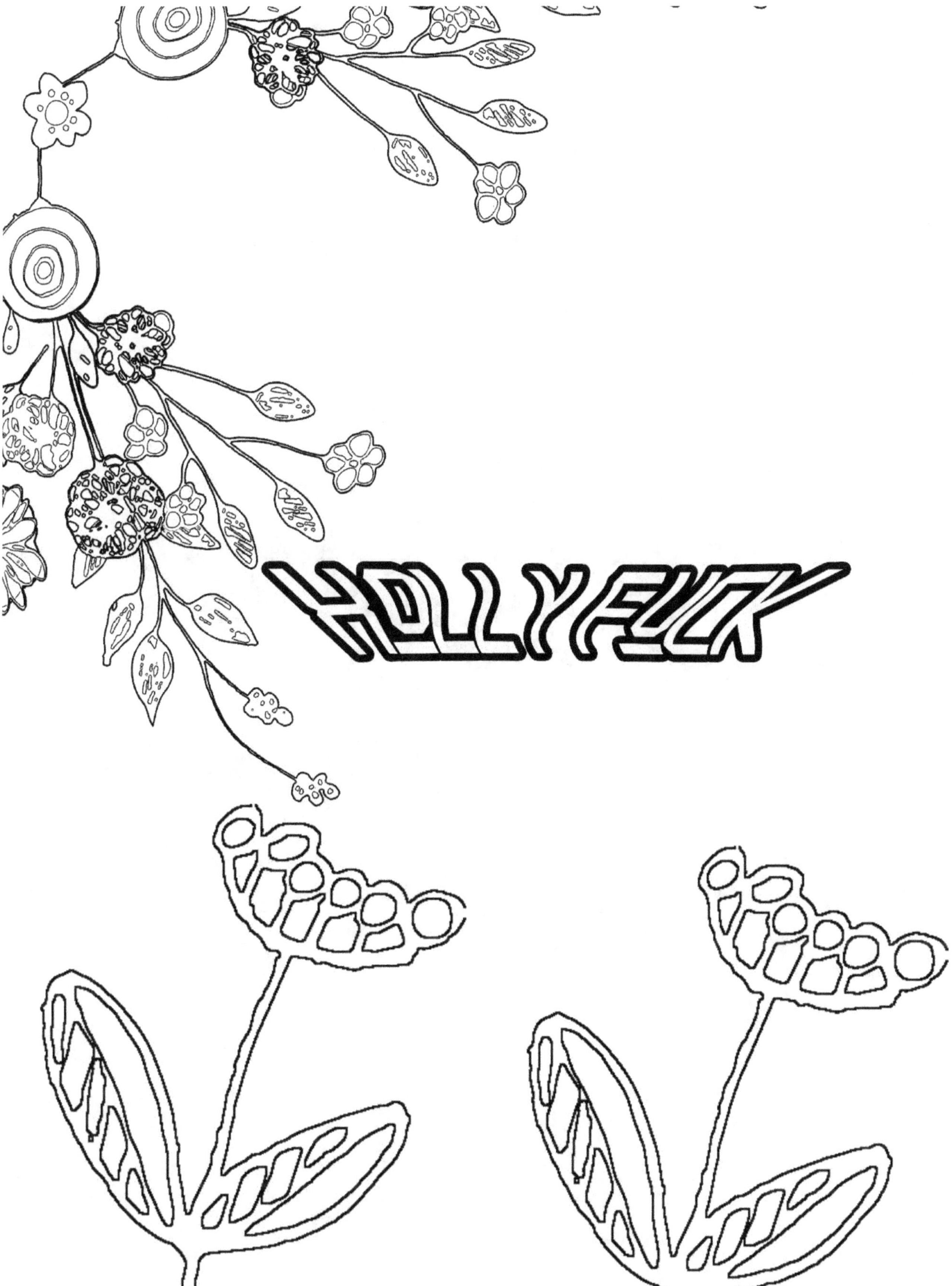
HOLLYFUCK

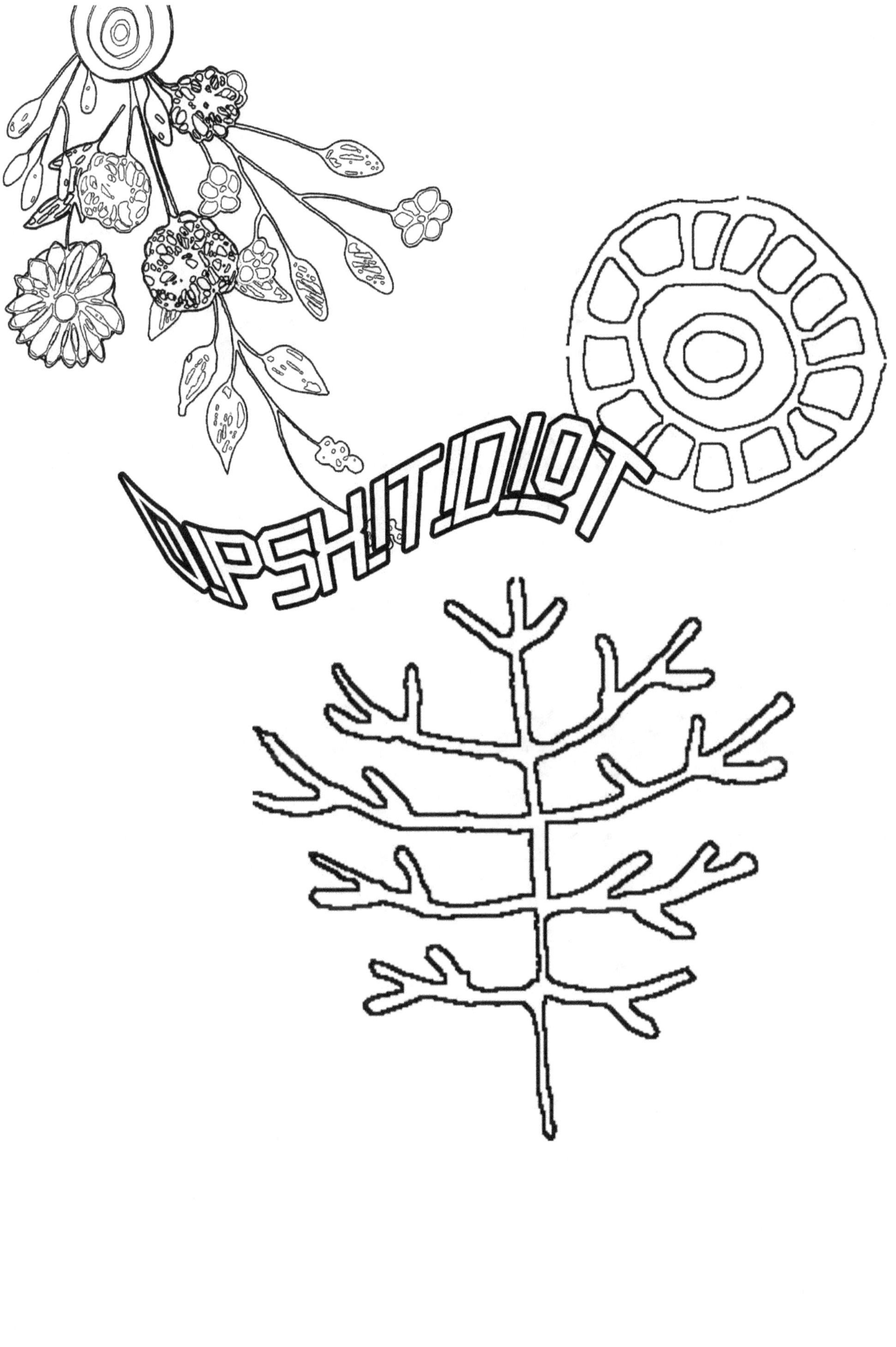
DIPSHIT IDIOT

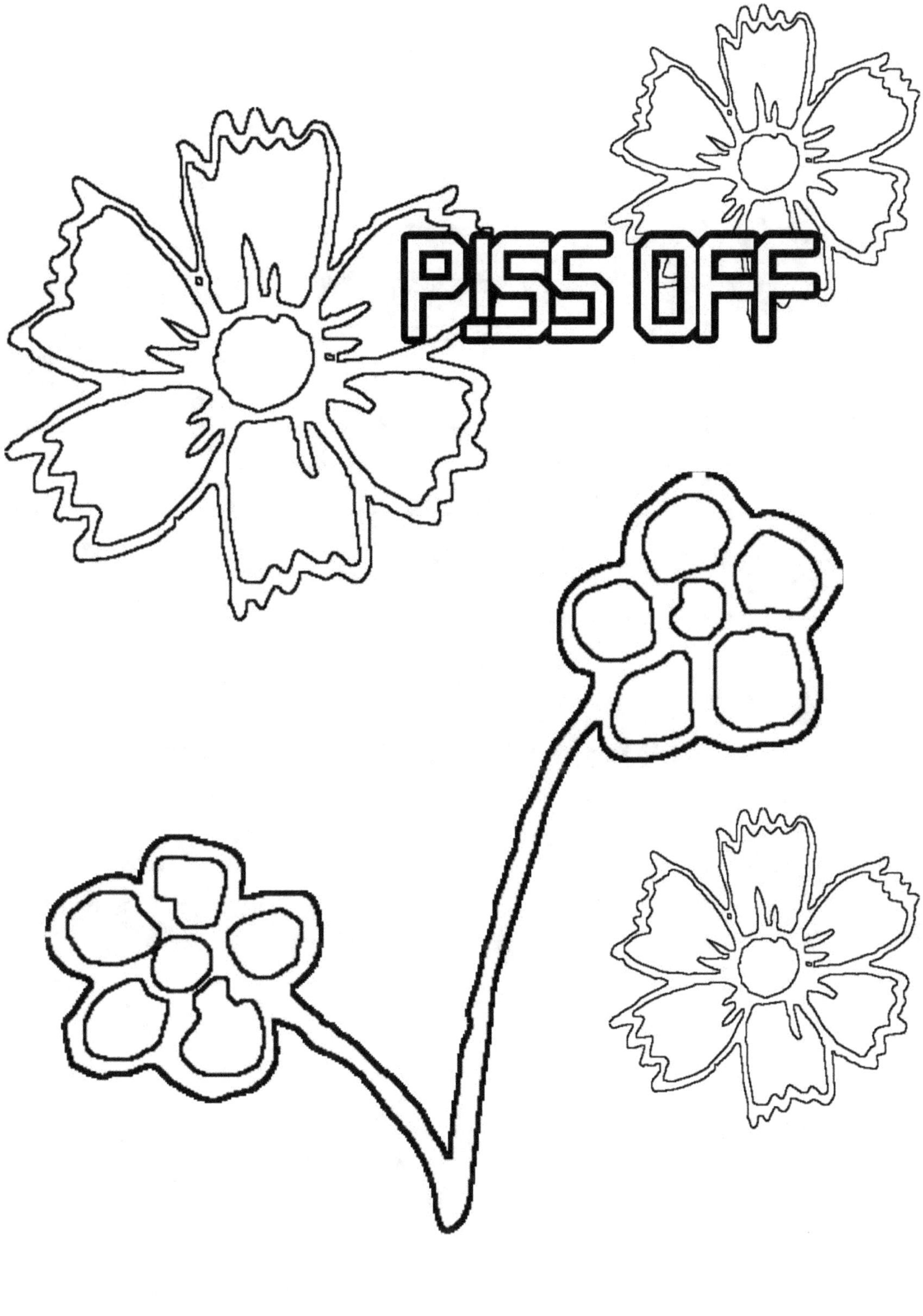
PISS OFF

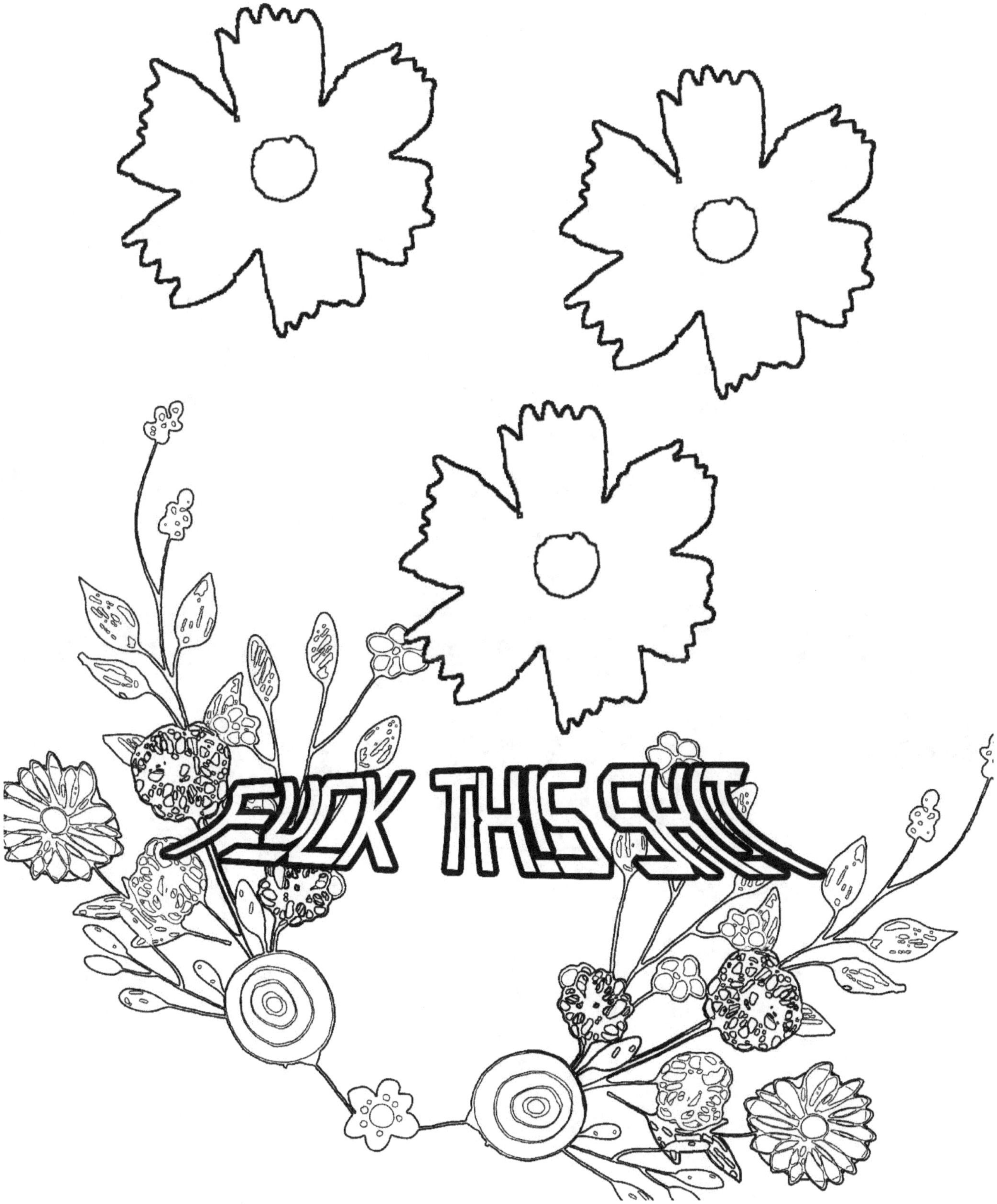
FUCK THIS SHIT

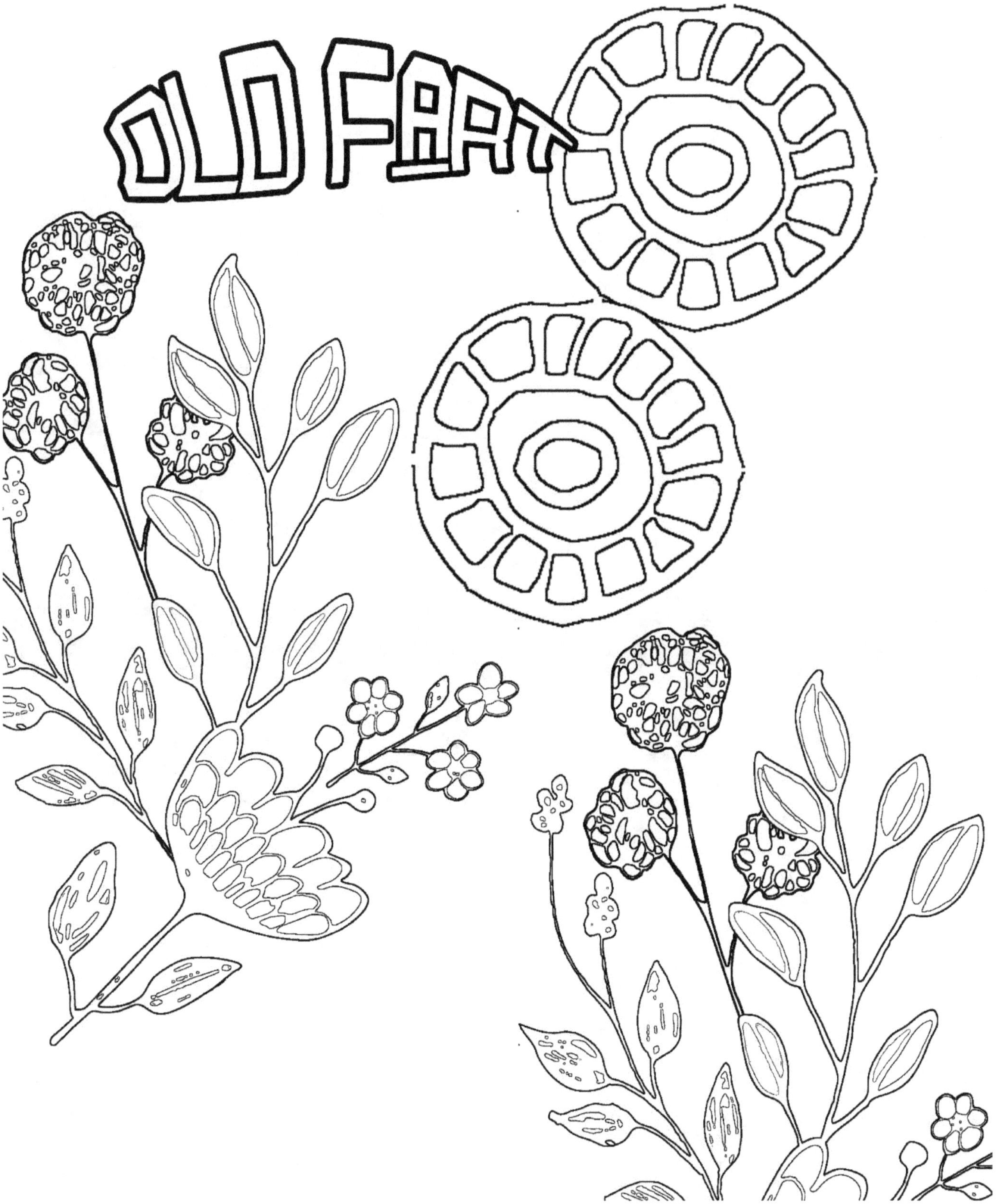
OLD FART

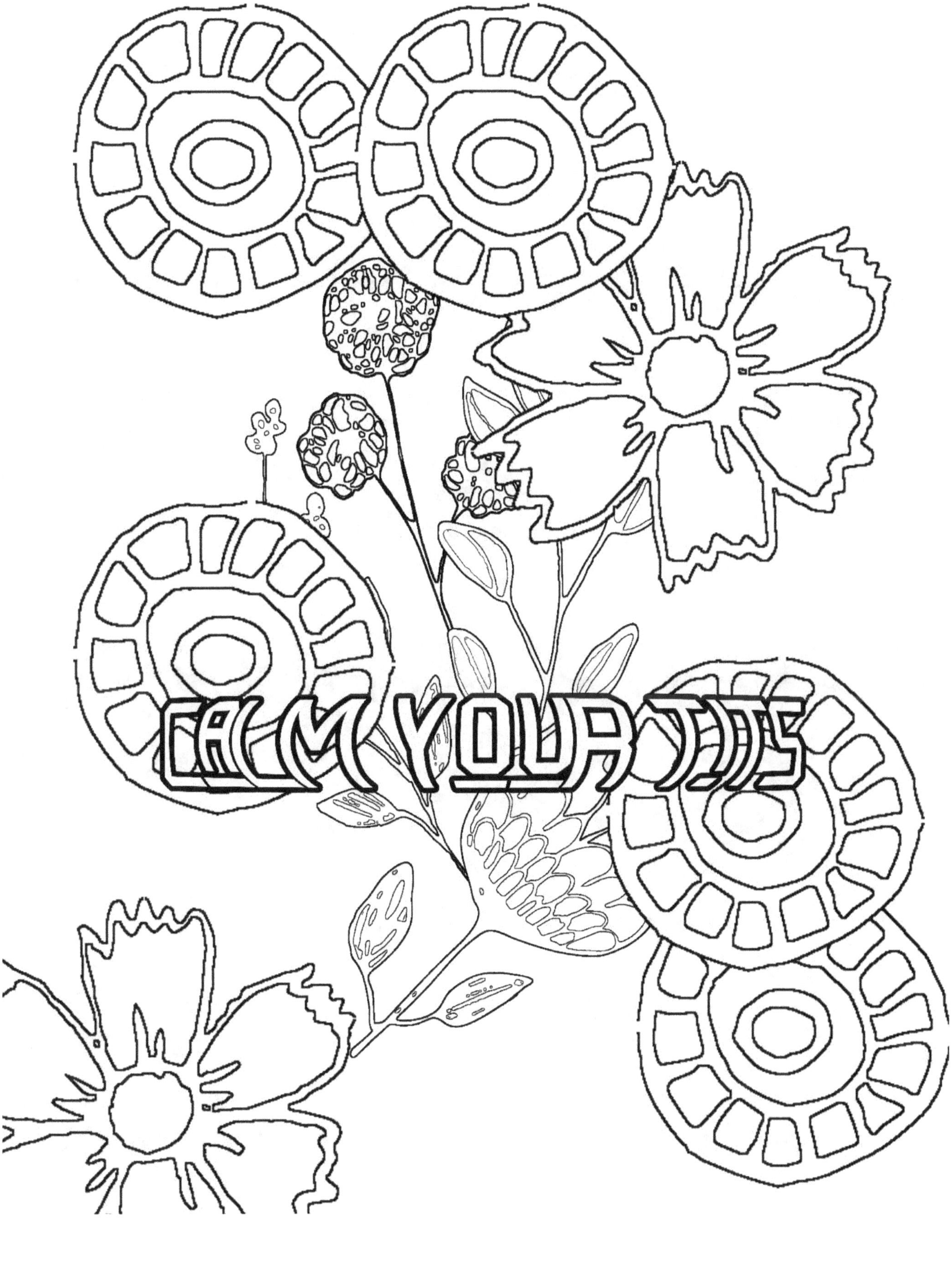
CALM YOUR TITS

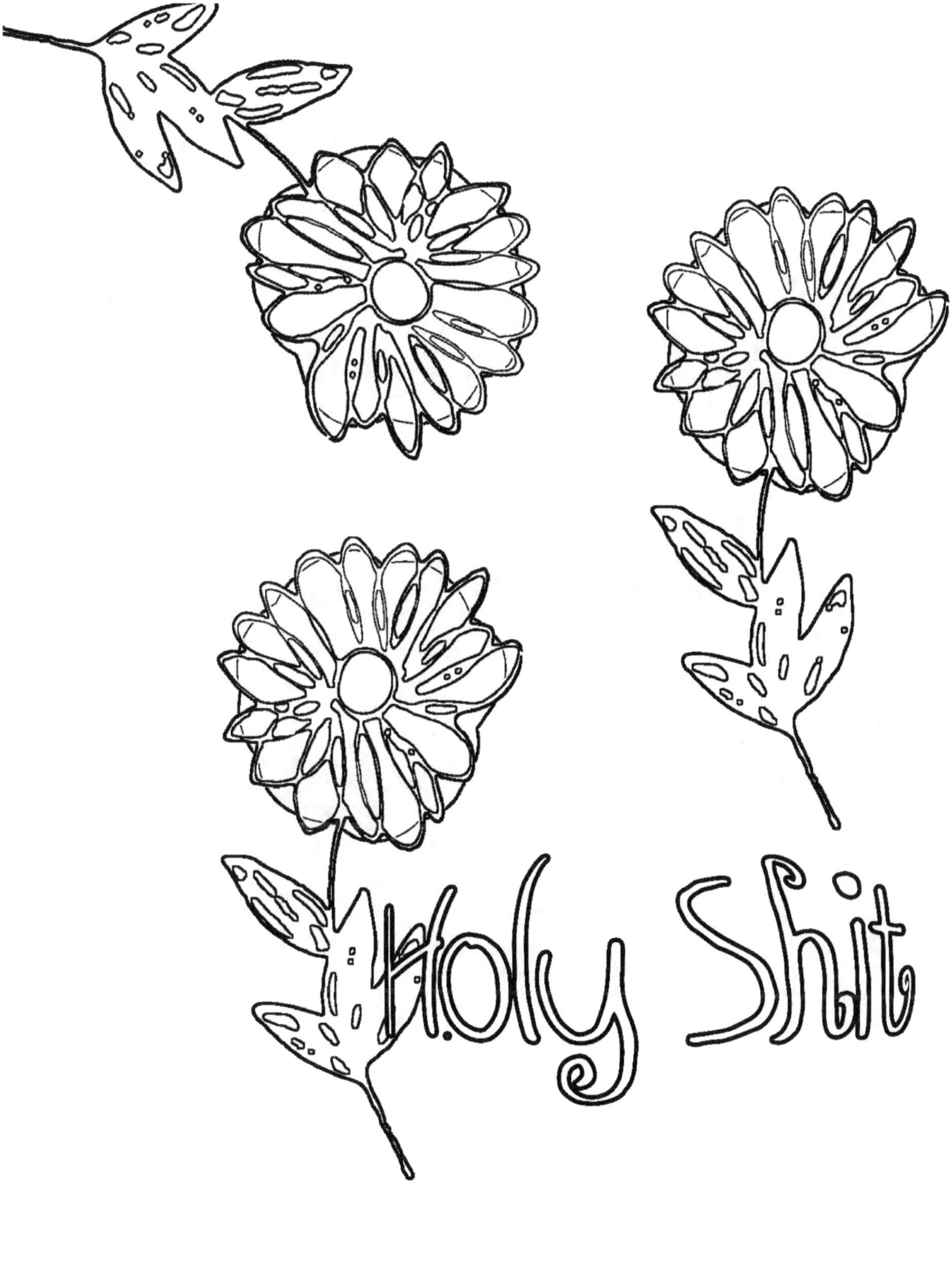
Holy Shit

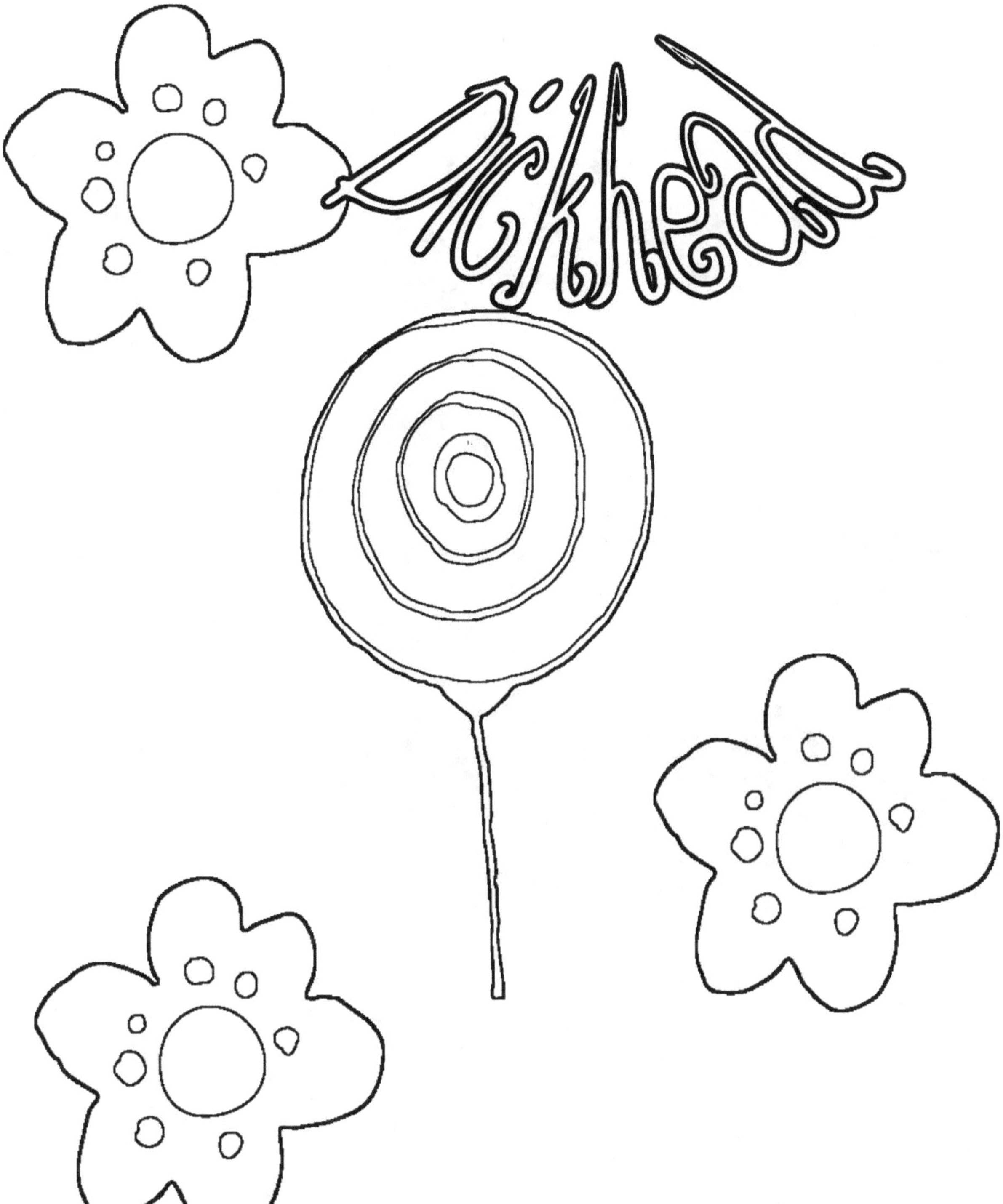
Dickhead

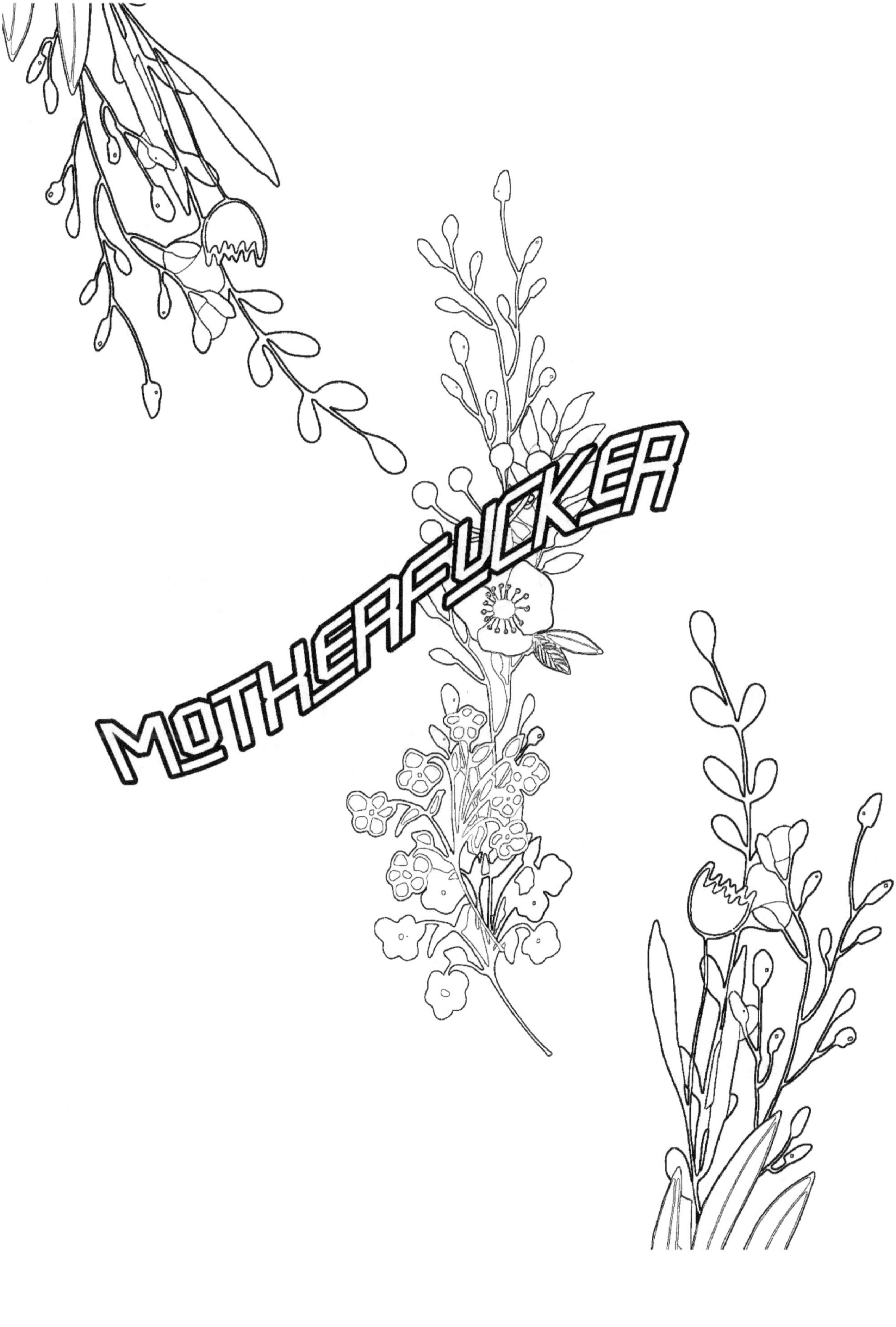
MOTHERFUCKER

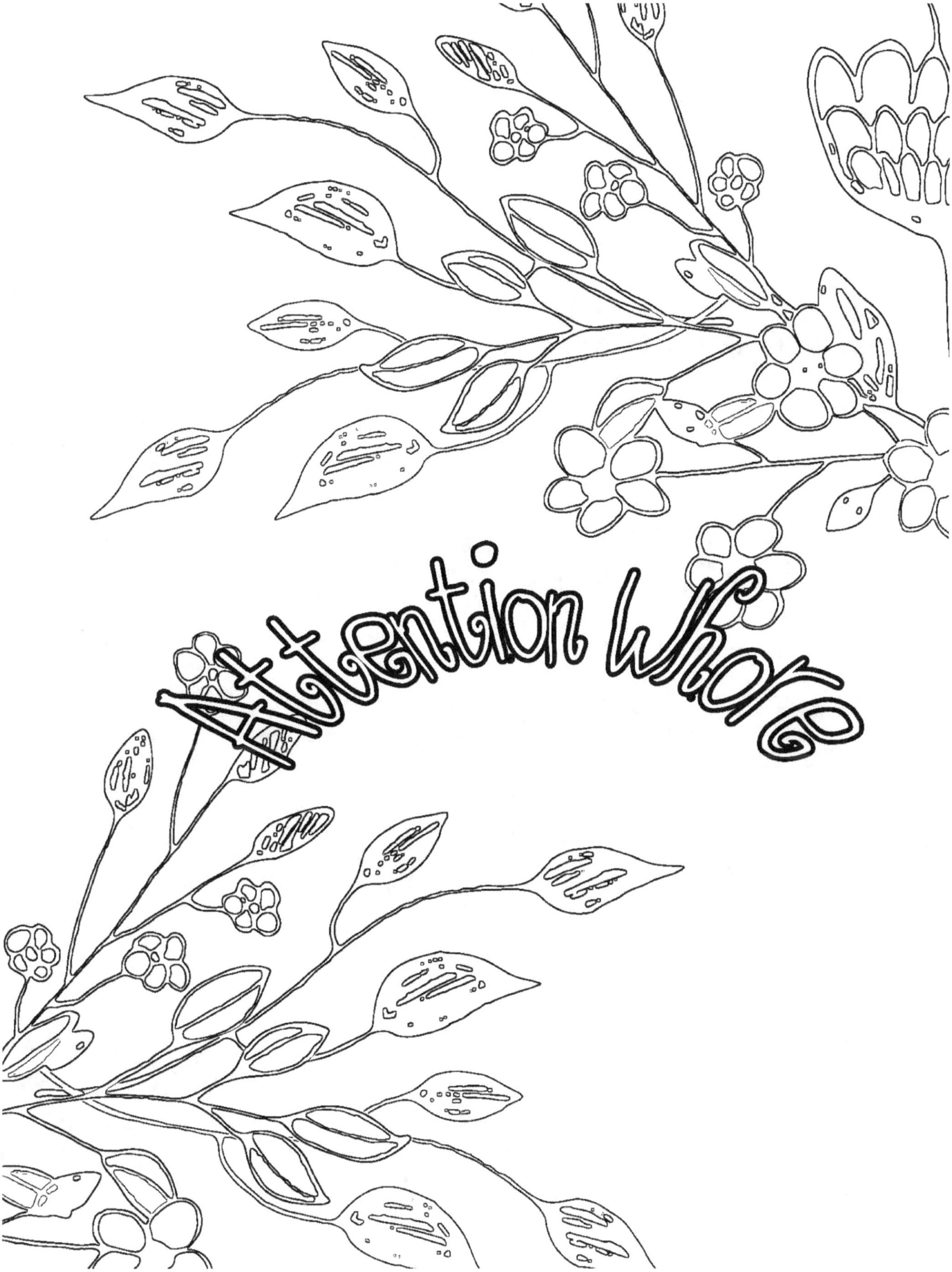
Attention Whore

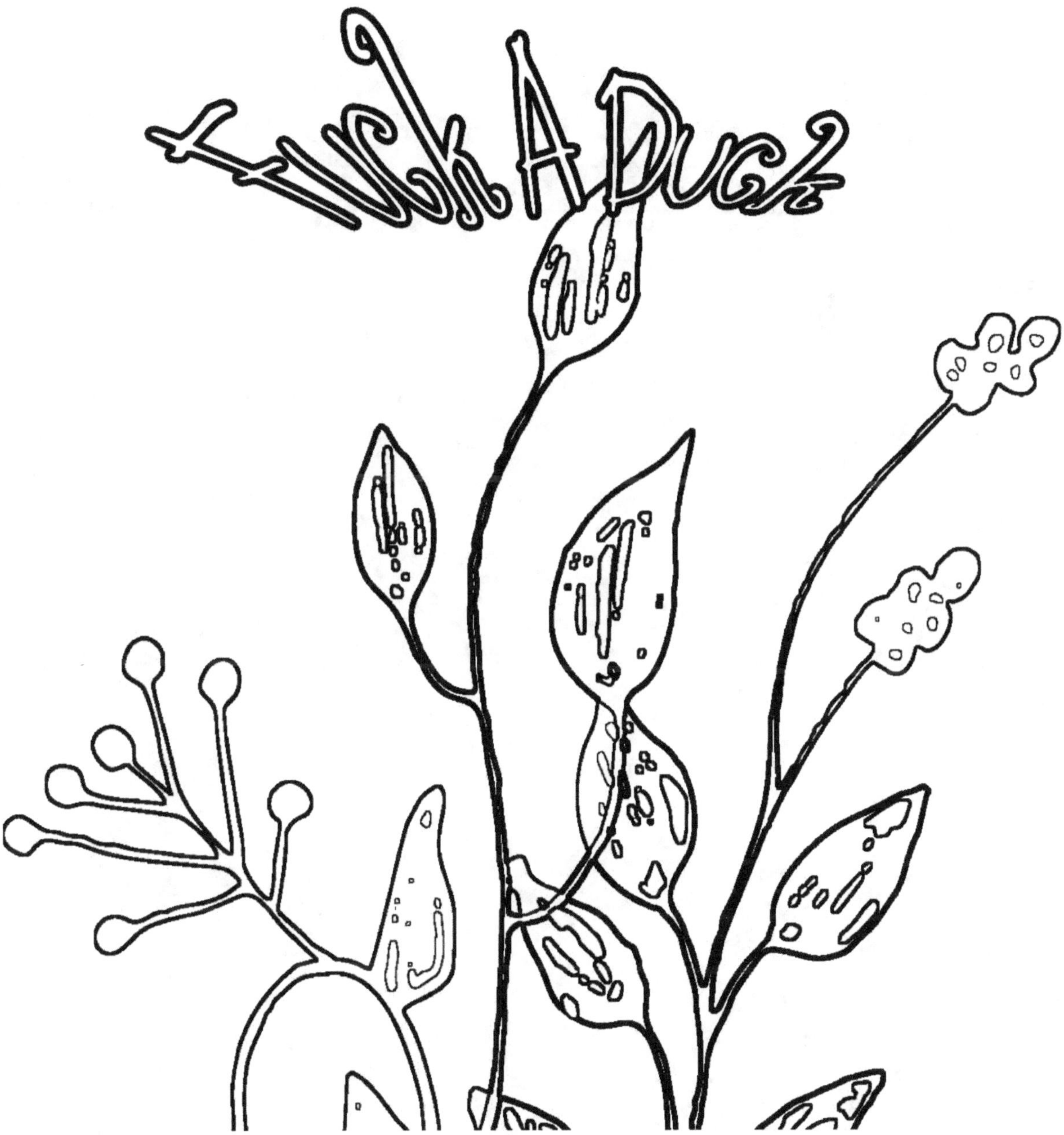
Fuck A Duck

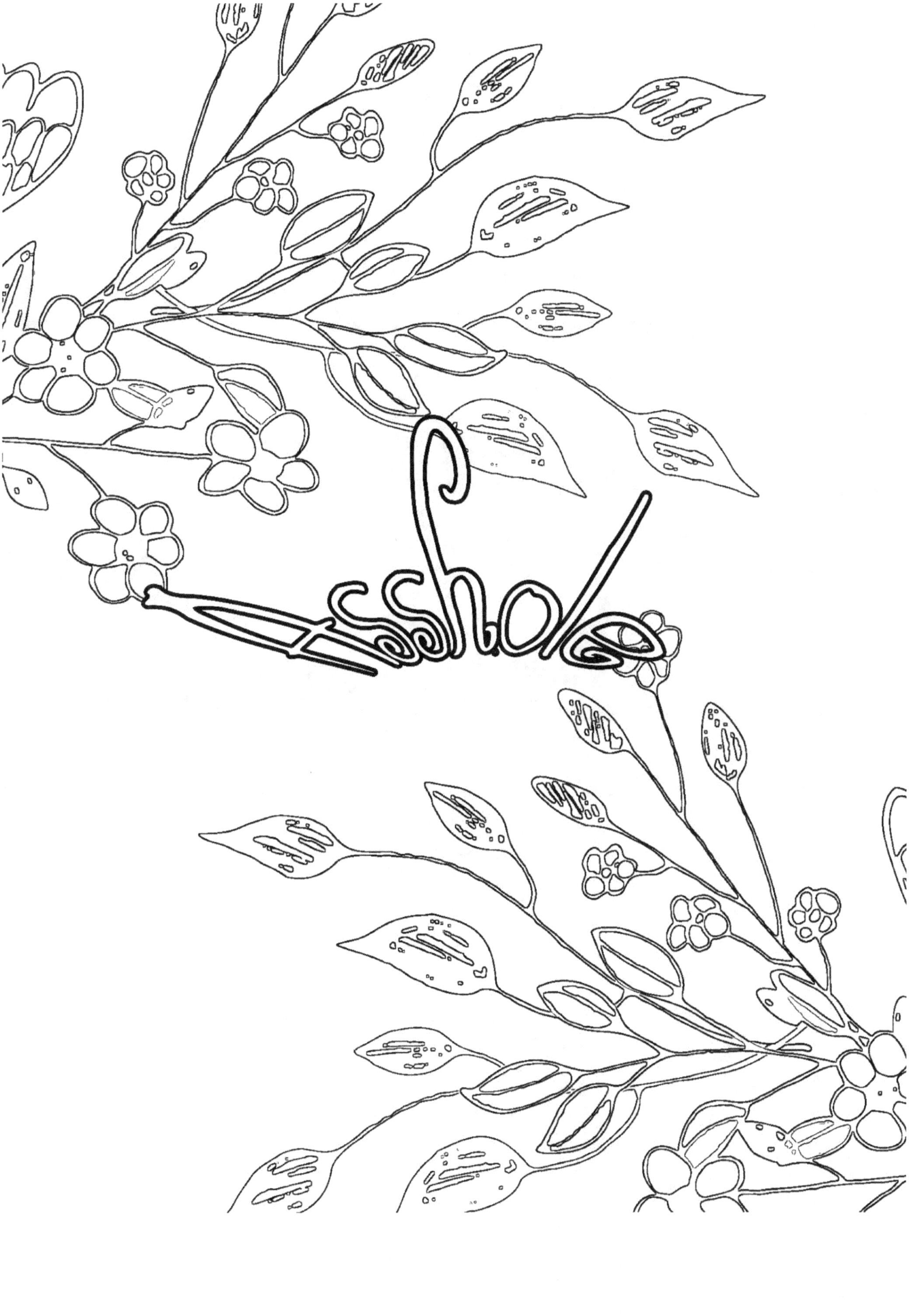
Asshole

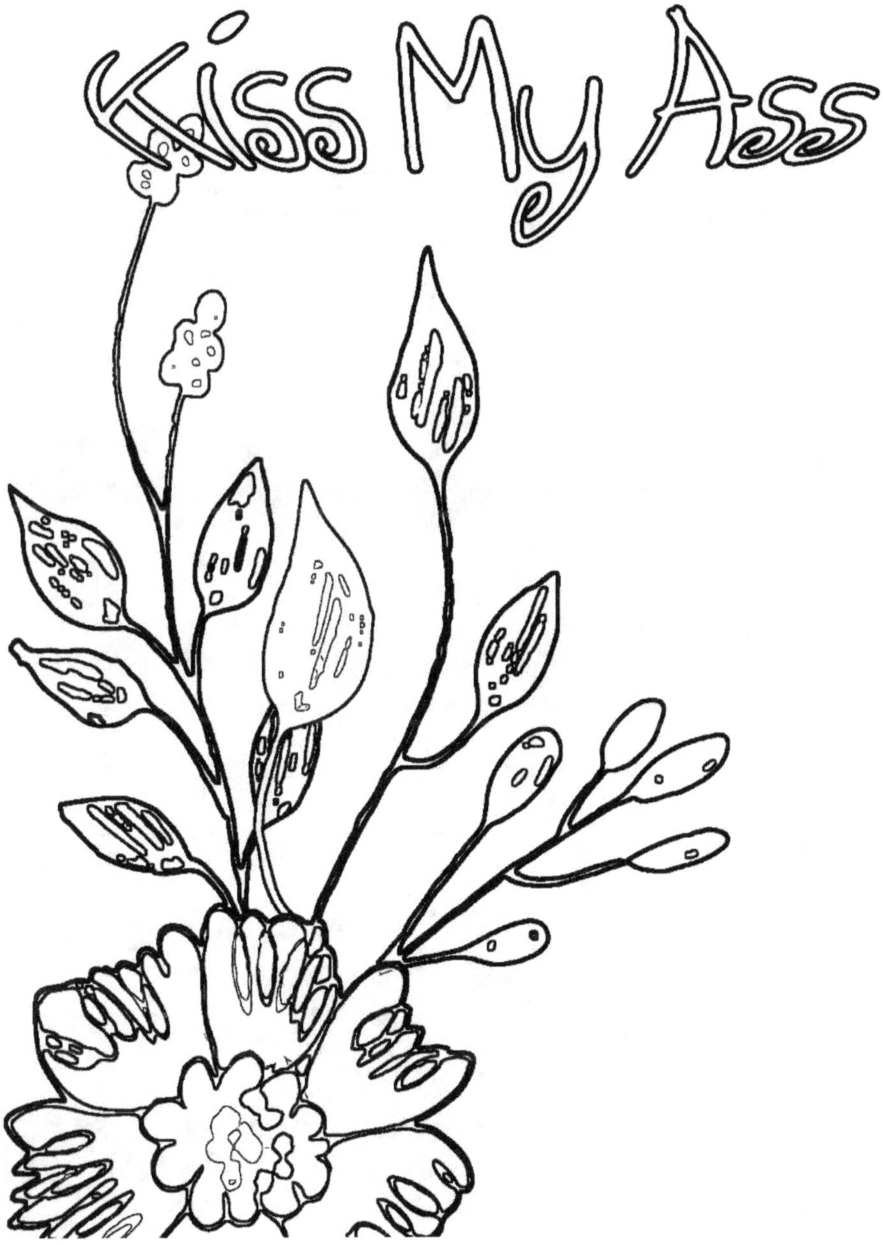
Kiss My Ass

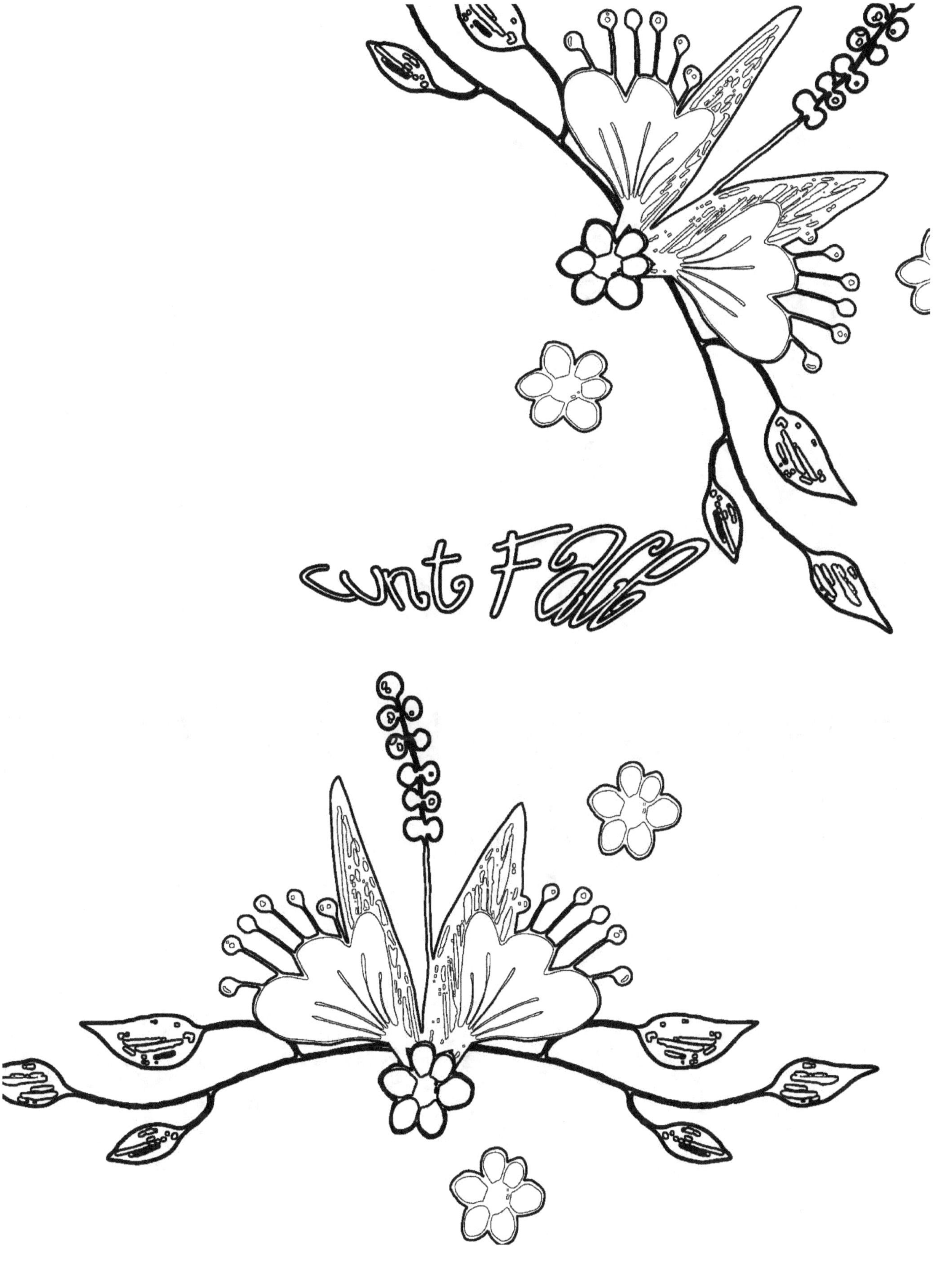
cunt

Cock & Balls

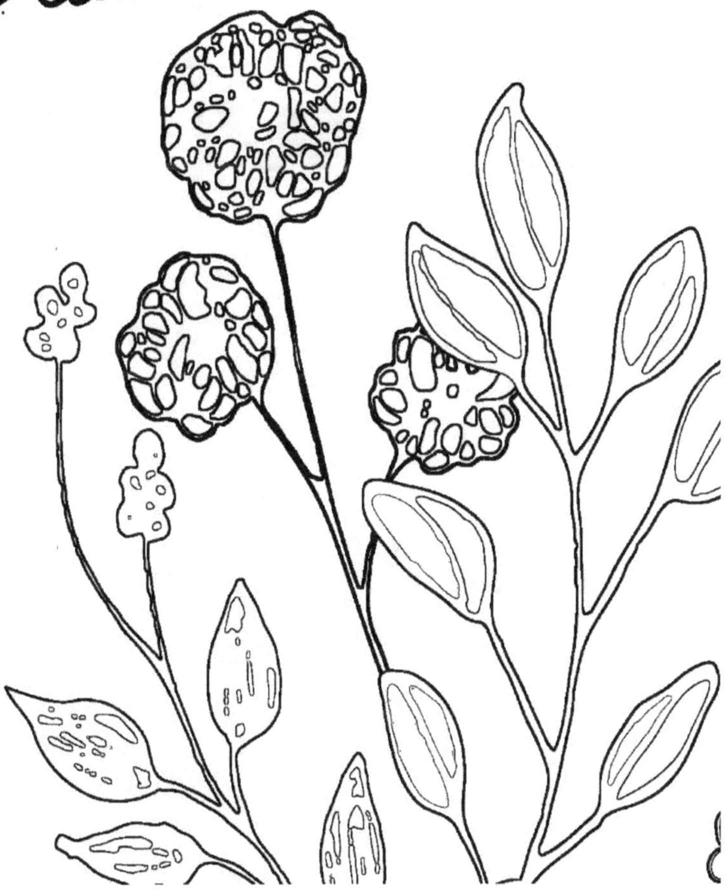

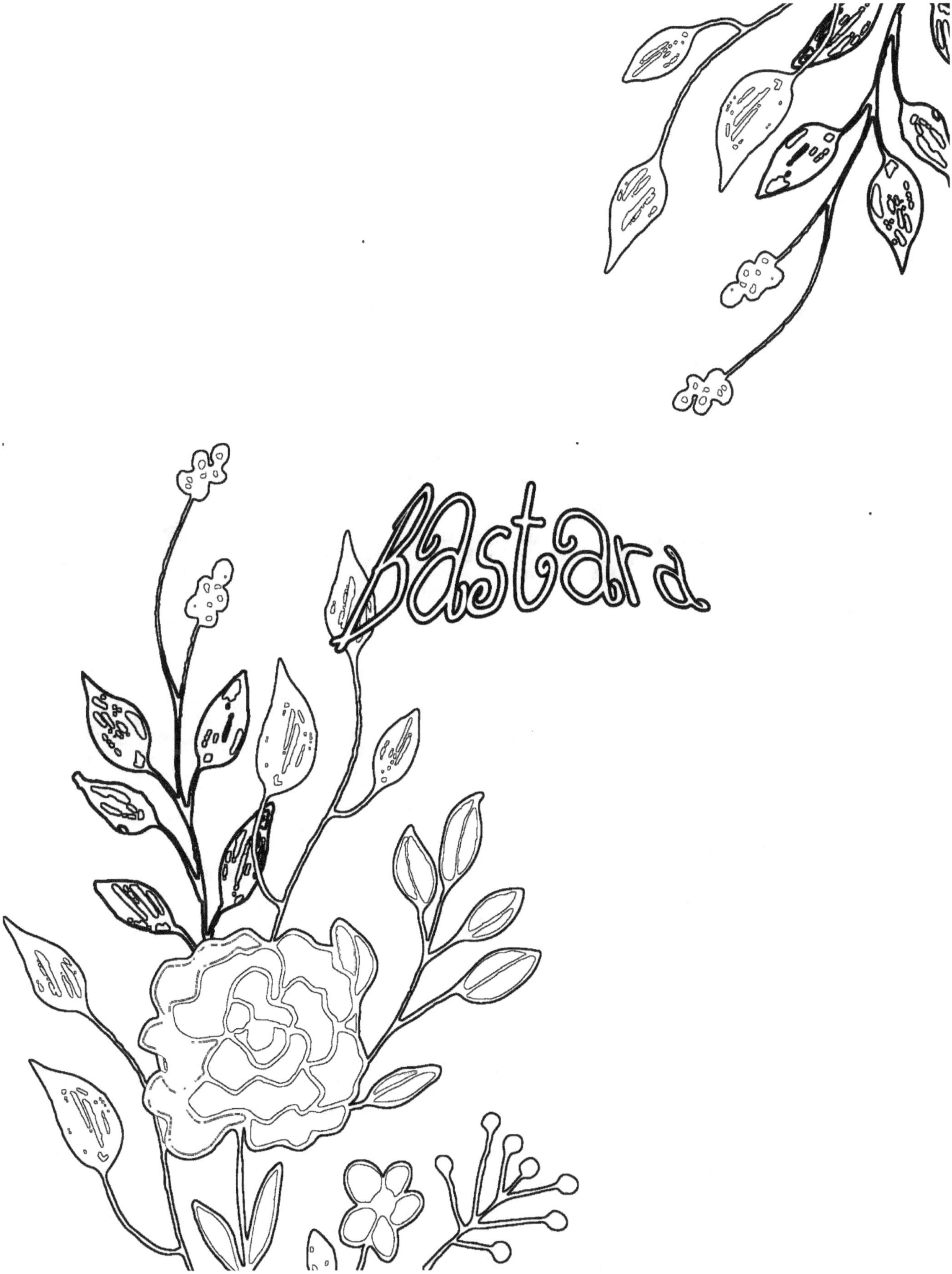
Bastarda

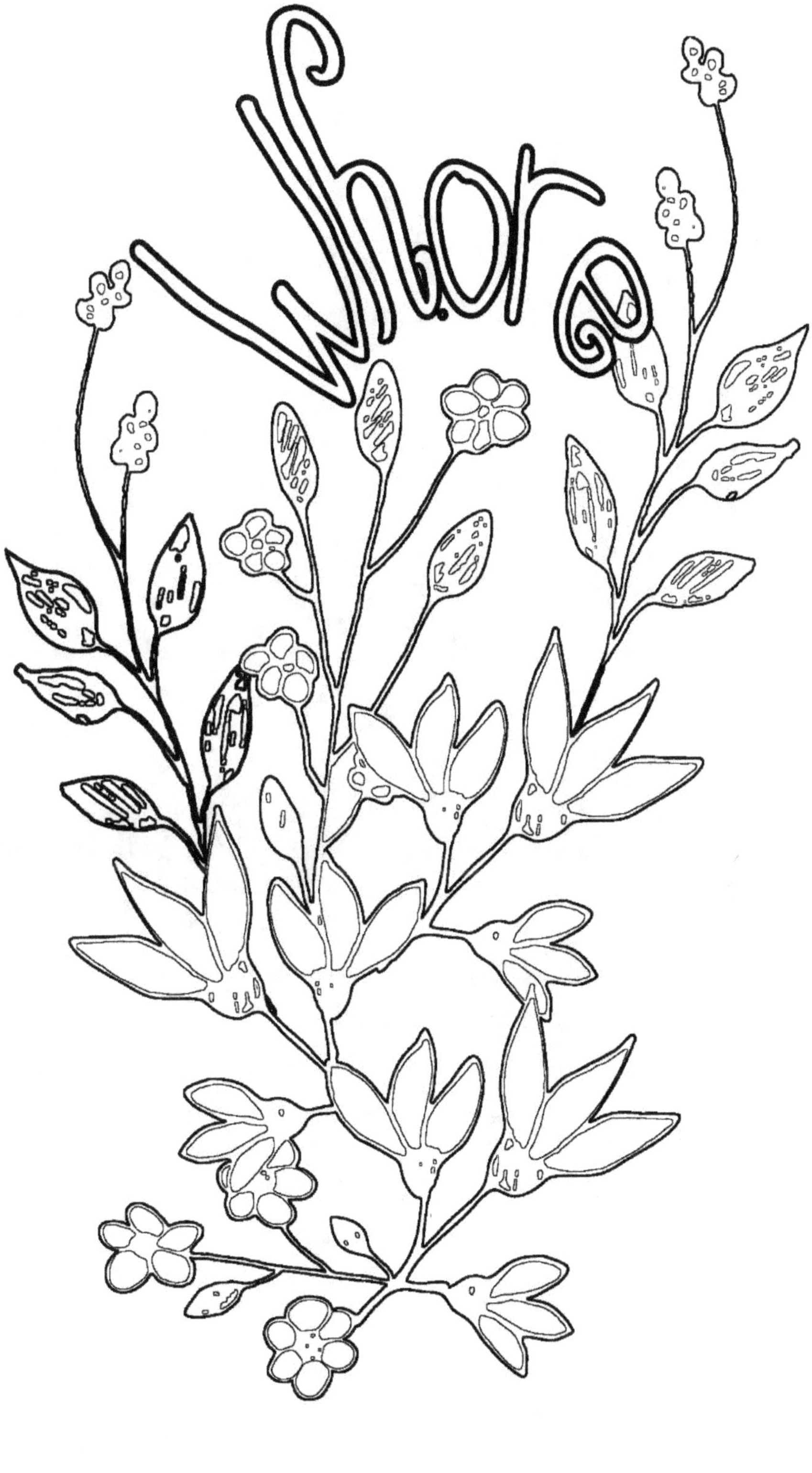
Whore

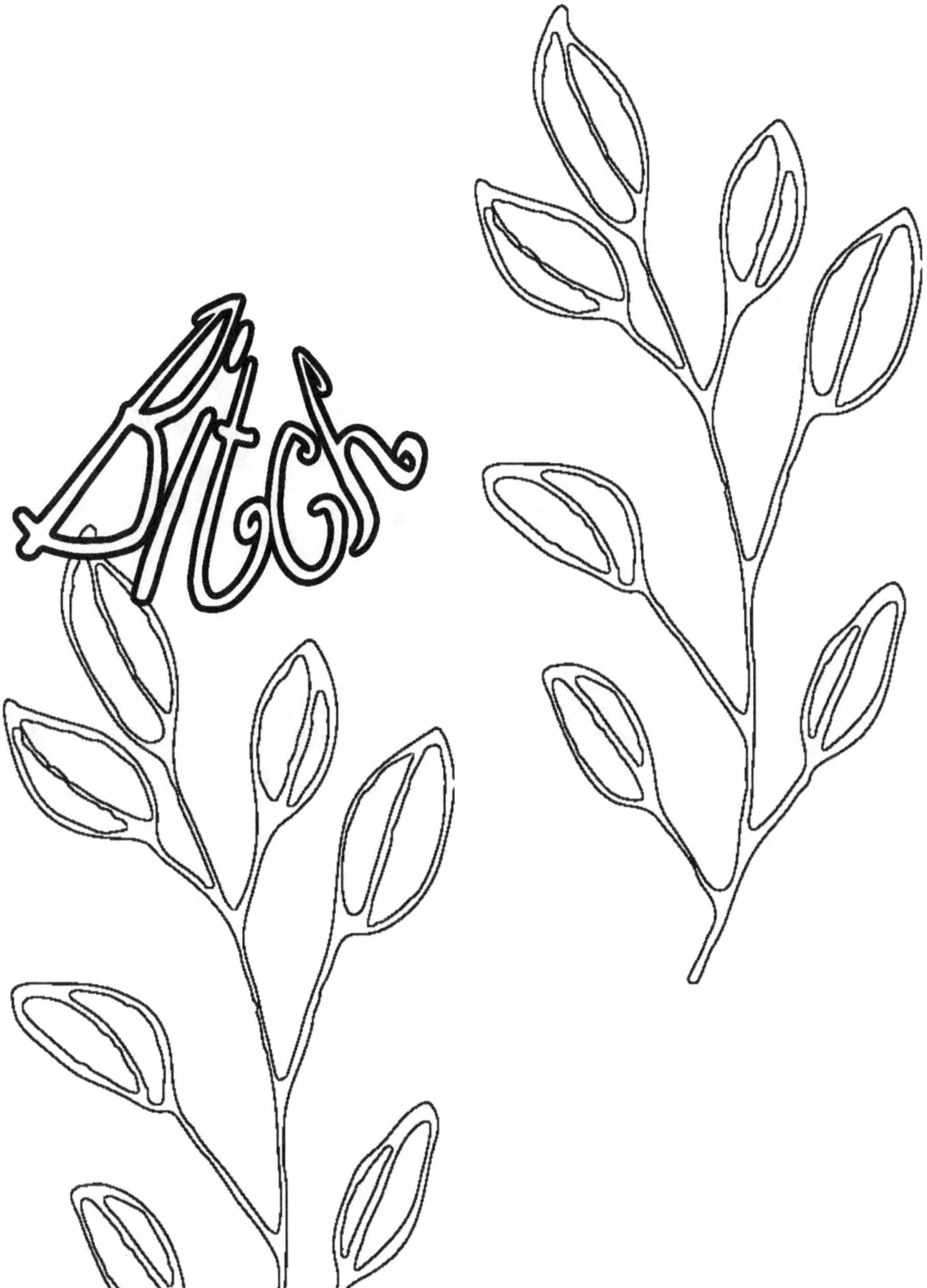
Bitch

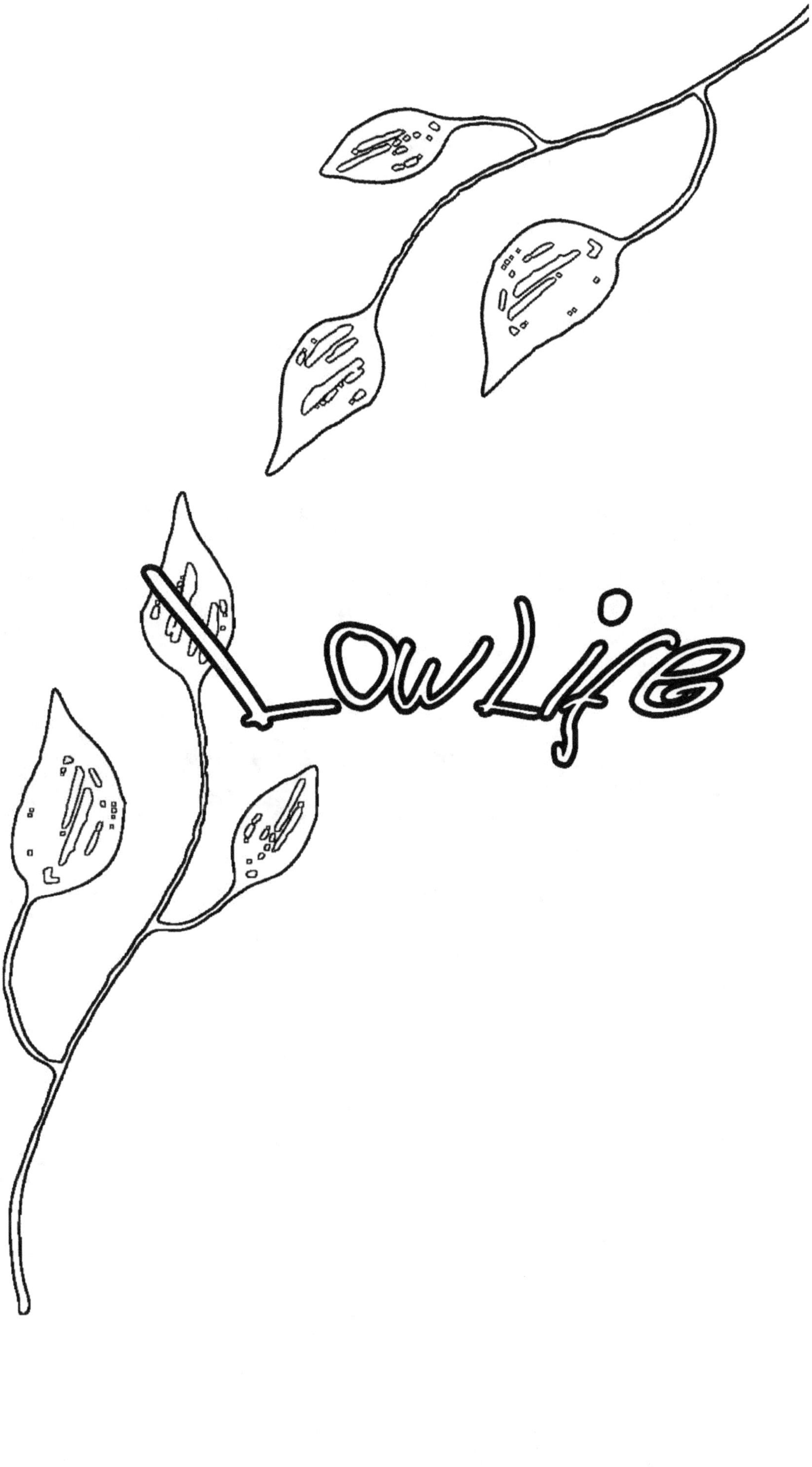
Low Life

www.ingramcontent.com/pod-product-compliance
Lightning Source LLC
Chambersburg PA
CBHW081748170526
45167CB00009B/3960
* 9 7 8 1 5 4 2 8 0 9 9 6 2 *